C000078253

Recognition In Modern Media

An Academic Essay

T.J. Johnson

First published by T.J. Johnson 2023

Copyright © 2023 by T.J. Johnson

All rights reserved. No part of this publication may be reproduced, stored or transmitted in any form or by any means, electronic, mechanical, photocopying, recording, scanning, or otherwise without written permission from the publisher. It is illegal to copy this book, post it to a website, or distribute it by any other means without permission.

T.J. Johnson asserts the moral right to be identified as the author of this work.
T.J. Johnson has no responsibility for the persistence or accuracy of URLs for external or third-party Internet Websites referred to in this publication and does not guarantee that any content on such Websites is, or will remain, accurate or appropriate.

Designations used by companies to distinguish their products are often claimed as trademarks. All brand names and product names used in this book and on its cover are trade names, service marks, trademarks and registered trademarks of their respective owners. The publishers and the book are not associated with any product or vendor mentioned in this book. None of the companies referenced within the book have endorsed the book.

First edition

Dedicated with gratitude and thanks to my great friend and intellectual muse: Rose Williams.

Contents

Foreword	ii
BOOK I	1
BOOK II	13
BOOK III	35
BOOK IV	58
BIBLIOGRAPHY	81

Foreword

Recognition in modern media lends itself to beginning to question and shed light on the problems of Profit Publishing. The subject of publishing, especially publishing in the modern age, was something which was not widely talked about, despite the publications being the ones responsible for this downfall in literature. Given this, it is unsurprising that T.J. Johnson decided to write an essay on this matter.

Johnson began writing this essay in March of 2021 when the world was in lockdown and home reading found itself in an uprise for the first time in many years. This begged for a higher understanding of what one was reading as the most popular books were influenced and pushed by various social media and because these books were popular, a unanimous agreement came that they must be well-written and well-received. But, though merely finishing a book is a great feat, it does not mean that the book is well written or worthy of the validation it received. A majority of this widespread success of certain books, Johnson deliberated, was due to a nepotistic eye in the media or an unquestionable eye for that which was to be published would be highly profitable. Though profit is important to a business, Johnson stated that it should not come at the expense of cognitive thought.

The idea of well-written literature has always been something T.J. Johnson has held tight in his mind and understanding how to read, write and understand well-written literature goes alongside that. A dogmatic belief of what well-written literature is would be the beginning of the downfall as it would narrow in on a style without allowing for change. On the other hand, allowing too much creative freedom and intellectual liberties would create a population of overly praised individuals who regard all of their works as great while the majority of it is mediocre or devoid of life. It is a fine line which publishers must draw. But the level bar which was set in place has fallen and now most books are published purely for profit and are chosen by the publishers on this basis. Johnson theorised, although this is not shown in the essay, that the publications should be taken by a committee and overseen and reviewed by the general public who are interested in reading. When this was placed into practice the results were varied. He found that the majority of readers, all given the same book which neither of them had read, found the book to be entertaining and wonderful. When questioned why they thought this, they replied that it was because they had heard of the writer before and they had heard they were humorous. This was not the case as the book was poorly written and had many spelling, and grammar errors with plot holes regarding no second read-through.

Johnson understood that this would not suffice as a method for choosing publication material as the general public had already had their ideas altered. Nor could he only use a selection of people who he had chosen to review as this would go against his idea of writing in a wider aspect. Johnson ended the reader's program in December 2022 due to varied results and an unsolvable dilemma regarding the readers.

Recognition In Modern Media was originally meant to be published in February of 2023, but due to Johnson's ideals of literature, he thought the essay was not ready and continued to work on it for another four months.

Despite all his differential and highly contended, attitude towards publishing, Johnson still forwards his point that publishing should be taken on a case-by-case basis, although it is unclear by whom, and that the publishers are at fault for the downfall of modern literature.

T.J. Johnson was born on the 7th of February 2005 in Leicestershire and was given a standard education in the local schools. It was when he began secondary school in 2016 that Johnson started showing a keen interest in literature, fiction at this point, saying that books were, "easier to read than humans". Although he did find friends in his school, he grew further and further from them as the school years went on and eventually cut his ties with a majority of them.

When T.J. Johnson was in year 11, and the age of 16, he began reading Russian literature in lou of fiction finding it more enticing due to, as he put it: "Their bleak nature and real-life attitude rather than silencing the ideas which they do not want to be voiced." This love for harder literature spread into a want to learn philosophy and psychology to better understand the world and its people.

Since then, Johnson has been the author of many published essays and short stories focusing on his philosophical beliefs such as death, consciousness, and human nature. He credits his interest in understanding man's mind to his Autism which he was diagnosed with at an early age. Johnson is credited with saying, "Humans are unpredictable, most books are predictable, but I cannot live amongst books for all my life so I must learn to live amongst people. I study them in the same way that Attenborough studies unknown species: by sitting quietly and taking notes."

BOOK I

CHAPTER 1
Introduction to the Subject of Profit Books

Good writing is not just by its actions but by its intentions and its meaning regarding the betterment of mankind. A good or well-rounded writer is merited from their actions, and it is from these actions that humanity betters itself. For many of the intellectuals, they will hold the subject of writing and reading books in high regard as they understand the profundity and importance of what they hold. While I recognize, as many like-minded people shall, that change is something that is inevitable in all things, this change should only be warranted by a need for change rather than a want for change in literature. Many more people will have it said that a change in literature should happen at the same time as the means of lifestyle change in the modern world. But it is also the world that has lost its principles and must change. And it is due to a modern, fast-paced change, that a downfall in modern academic society has been dragged down with it. Therefore, it is not change that we should be concerning ourselves with, but instead concerning ourselves with the principles of writing well rounded literature.

Sometimes writers will create a book purely for capital gain and the name that comes with it. These books I have coined under a new sector called Profit Books. When the author has attempted to write a book, short story or essay and only written or picked a genre/ storyline which they know will sell: that is a Profit Book. They never intended to write what was in their emotions as this would have led to an uproar of angry readers. Instead, they chose to write on a subject that they understood would give them a good title and sell well. These books most commonly focus on the genres of romance, modern sexuality and magical fiction. When, the writer should be focusing on philosophy, questioning and higher learning. Granted, the author may choose to write what he/she wishes to, but it is important to remember that one cannot lie to oneself about what one likes and dislikes.

A book can be classified as a Profit Book only after it has been read. If the book was read and seemed bland, devoid of colour life and plot, then it can be classified as a Profit Book. For example, if a graphic designer were to create a poster and was only thinking solely about the payment at the end, then this would inevitably show in the final piece. It would be understood that it seems bland, and the designer could have done more. This phenomenon occurs when authors write Profit Books. The same can be said for literature. Profit Books create a platform of unrememberable characters and plot lines where once the book is finished, there is to be no more attenuation of mental definition and no more insightful reading. Once it is finished, it is finished both mentally and physically.

In the modern world most books are written as Profit Books. The agenda by which we live means that most writers cannot afford to live by normal modern standards. Thus, the standards of writing have also changed. I always state that a person should write because they are human, but modern agendas state that goods and services cost money. This means that, like in many professions, people must change what their meaning of an ideal life is to a life that is better suited to supporting themselves, a household, and possibly a family. That is why most modern literature is written as Profit Books.

This shift in the culture of literature is also changing how books are read and written. The characters are becoming more two-dimensional as well and the plot lines are rushed and cliche. This also changes how they are read. Most adults now consider that they read a lot when they are reading books with larger print words to make them seem like a larger book. Rather than larger and more complex language that will push their boundaries of reading and understanding of the world around them, if not further out than that. The language and imagery used also suggest that most of these books can be read and understood by all ages and are not written for certain groups of people. This creates more potential for free enterprise in capital for the author but at the loss of the mental structure of the readers. The readers are reading books that can be read by all ages, therefore there is no mental attenuation in unpacking what they have read: therefore, no critical mental development.

CHAPTER 2
Admission to the Media

When in the field of writing it seems that many people are pushed forwards and have all the benefits of publishing while others do not. This can be down to many factors. Some benefit because of the title they hold in life. This will allow them to gain nepotistic capricious advantage for a writing domain with extensive injustice against the common and smaller writer. It is very hard to believe that all celebrity writers are learned in the literary arts and spent years mulling over unpublished drafts before publishing their first novel biography, or essay.

Certain authors are praised in their field and others are not so much. Two books, which we will call the first X and the other which we will call Y, shall be compared to one another. X has well-paced scenes, and well-developed characters and is written with an air of confidence which conveys trust in the author's words.

Y, being written at the same time and is the same length, has no plot development, very two-dimensional characters, and a constantly changing voice insecure of itself. So why is it that Y is being pushed forward in publication and X is not? This is because Y has had the effect that most modern literature has on the public which is easy readability. An average person will choose the easier-to-read piece of literature over the harder as for the obvious reason stated.

Due to television and the ever-growing and faster-consuming media, everything in life is spoon-fed to a generation of modern adults who feel no need to think for themselves. This is the de-saturation of media and the concepts for which it stands for trying to appeal to many so that it loses its plot and will never-the-less succeed in failing itself as an enigmatic shenanigan of buzzwords and diluted stories: this is the Profit-Booking industry-made film. A book, though, which can feed them basic words, plot and characters is to be as highly praised, if not more so, as the man who first went to the moon. An overindulgence in the silent majority and overbearingly loud minority, have stipulated the world we live in to condone actions such as writing a book to be great feats. That is correct. The book, when written correctly and in the proper fashion, is a great and mammoth feat. But it is not so when the feat is rushed, uncoordinated and in a state of constant tone shift. A man should grow to understand the importance of knowing when a piece of work is for pleasure of self and self only, or for the world and all who indulge in greatness.

CHAPTER 3
Rejection From the Media

Meanwhile, most authors do not get published or pushed forward in their writing due to, once again, who they are. This selective classism of the literary mind creates a bias toward those who have great ideas, not to share them. A publisher will most likely choose to publish the more famous person's essay or short story over the less well-known one. And so how are people ever supposed to get a start in the publishing world if these are the standards by which they must compete? This classist behaviour was prevalent in Russia during the 1890s and caused many to starve and give up on their ideas purely due to never being given a chance to gain a platform. This was serfdom. While not so severe in the publishing world, the ethics and behaviour of the classes are primarily the same.

Unrealistic expectations can cause a person to fail, and that is to say "fail" very vaguely as even a few book sales are a success in their publication process. This overachiever and marginalized view of top writers and editors sets the average bar - in the mind- very low and will perplex and warp the image of anyone who can sell a book with little experience. For if it's written and out there, it will have to be a bestseller. This is the common thought of the uneducated writer.

When there is too little planning placed into the manuscript there will be complications in what is done later. If, for whatever reason, there were to be little planning placed into the manuscript; it shows too little planning of mentality and a naive mind. This disability causes people to fail in their works getting published, but they will consequently blame others for their mistake's poor choices and lack of understanding claiming themselves as the "underappreciated genius" who is yet to be discovered: This is the mind of a narcissistic writer.

But not all processes in publishing are to be blamed on the writer: some are to be cornered and scoped on the publisher. Profit margins have to be maintained as also the reputation and betterment of the company. For this reason, many publishing houses, when faced with an influx of manuscripts, will tend to take from the corner of certain reasoning in choosing to publish books by established names rather than from the corner of uncertain reasoning in new and upcoming authors. This is, of course, a mere showing of what business is in the twenty-first century. But from which can the flames rise if the ashes are scattered? There is more trust to be found in people with already published pieces through the company but who will be given the chance for succession if never given the opportunity?

CHAPTER 4
Roles of Influence in Modern Media

When reading, people individualize their scope of reading onto a certain genre or domain: Russian, French, fantasy, and sometimes even romance: mostly of different and underrepresented types of romance than the traditional sense. But it is in this that people will miss out on the wider view and knowledge that both modern and classical literature contains. By choosing to read from a limited and narrowed scope, people will only be opening their minds to the brief perspective that they wish to focus upon. Ludwig Wittgenstein stated: "The limits of my language are the limits of my mind." This simply proves that one cannot talk or open their intellect up as far if not without first seeking the absurd and different. By reading from a scope further than your own, your mind is, in turn, opened up to new ideas, writing prompts and structures, and even the tone or language in which it is written. It is for this reason that social media holds such power over the common man in literature.

Social media has dominated the Western world and is infiltrating their ways into Eastern culture as well. With over half the global population entranced by apps (59% as of 2022), it is not the individuals who will elect leaders, but the algorithm coders. People, on average as of September twenty twenty-two, spend nearly 4.8 hours, two-hundred and eighty-eight minutes, a day on their phones and 2.45 hours, one-hundred and forty-seven minutes of that on social media. And so, it is not the people creating content that choose the next president: it is, in fact, the algorithm coders.

With many people using social media as a primary form of news and knowledge intake, and the main demographic still having their minds critically developed, the type of stock placed on these sites will cause the next trend to appear in humanity one after the next. If books are to be that, or if there is a secret surplus of stock of shoes, the coder can, and most likely will - for the correct amount - rewrite their script to incorporate this new trend producing a higher pushing percentage of certain goods and services or alumni. With the naive majority wanting to be the same creatures of comfort they always were due to a fear of rejection, they will succumb to submission and consequently purchase or visit whatever it is off the site, only to post it later on a site and never actually use the tool they have ordered or seen. And it is due to these comforting creatures that the world refuses to change in its image. It is stated that the majority of the inhabitants of social media sites are people below the age of twenty-five, and this is the case. And it is these people who fear the rejection of their peers more so than any other more necessary fear: it is this that the officials desire for the reasoning of control. Persecution of an individual, absurd and free mind for the reasons of abolition in the realm of conformity is not to distinguish the injustices of the persecutor from past tragedies and intolerances but merely conform itself to a misunderstanding of individualism.

There is, of course, a science behind all of this as well as algorithms. But in the end, the people will almost always be the conformity creatures and the authorities a herring of deepest red bearing a delusional mask and facade for the true puppeteer. There will only be true salvation once the bonds and chains of the human mind on blue light are broken. It is only brief joy, not everlasting and never real: that comes from unhinged adventure.

But the principles of a library in the terms and confides of a computer should not in all of one bit be commandeered as an attack on the printed written word. As there is still much of the world bound by the grasp of illiteracy, talking books help them to understand the wisdom inside and appreciate what they could have learned if it were not for more dire needs. Also, in the time of worldwide economic crises, the pricing structure of digital books supports those who cannot afford books as whole paper and hardback structures. Reading, writing and learning is a human right that stands taller than any other, bringing untold possibilities. And the modern age can bring these humanitarian liberties to people who reside in all corners of the globe. The intrinsic liberties granted by such beings to, so few less fortunate souls are to grant destruction to the injustices and provide equal learning rights for all men and women.

BOOK II

CHAPTER 5
A Naked Decision

If I were to take the cover, spine and author name from the manuscript: would it still read the same? Critically, yes. But intrinsically, no. Because most people will read books due to the author's name or because they have been recommended the book to read at some point, it would be read differently and in a biased mind. If, as previously stated, I was to remove the title and the reader were to read the manuscript without bias of name or recommendation, they would come to an honest and pure conclusion on whether it is a well-written book or not.

In most cases, this would not suffice as the author would need to be given recommendations and services for their efforts in the manuscript. Most magazines and small publishers do read them in an unbiased setting, and this especially goes for competitions, but the manner from which I speak is from the perspective of novels and mainstream publishing.

On the opposite side of the same coin, it explores why such a method would not be as simple or as well executed an idea as one may initially think, and this is due to copyright and ownership. Someone could easily take the piece and call it their own and when the real owner is to arrive; they will have very little evidence to back up their statements. But to keep the title attached is not to remove injustice in the name of publication as the contract will still stand and give inconsistent mercurial advantages to the higher parties. Instead, the leading and following parties must agree on part-ownership or full ownership of the pieces granted for print.

Writing is a major form of expression and has been mastered by many. But many more mistreat this and feel that their expression is the best and the only good version. This is pure abuse on the subject. To further indulge in the whims of the meek and unfit regarding literature is to be destroying any meaning of life itself. A society built upon the whims of these immovable points is doomed to forever repeat itself and celebrate these repetitions as if they were individual geniuses.

If a book is distributed by the leading majority

party, the publishers, and owned by the following party, then the question arises of its value and importance in the modern world. Indeed, the common man is a fool and knows not what he wants but only knows what he desires. For the publication to be given any sort of credibility the laws on distribution without cover, name or detail are to be ensured. However, this is not feasible for the primary levels stated. Instead, the book must commit itself to killing off the excess detail whilst combining the name, title and companies included in the respective fonts, sizes and shapes necessary to the specific manufacturing processes and target. Punishment is to be claimed by the party who disagrees with the publication of knowledge processes either in a physical sense or in mental anguish. The book cover, title and gravitas are to be directed to the primary constituency involving the production of media for the amelioration of the mind. Never may it be used for the whims of the foolish and naive. To call a book anything else than what has been stated is supreme abuse to the men and women who have written their lives away for the whims of ideocracy.

Though to the learned mind the world is absurd and follows no set of boundaries than what the singular man placed there himself, there is still a right and a wrong. Religion states that there is a right and a wrong way to do every task and those rules have been ordained by a God. But, religious or not, every action has a consequence that will either legitimise or cancel it. A mind filled with the absurd must consider them to be calming. And the term "Calming" can be interchanged with "the best chance of rectification in man."

CHAPTER 6
Mixed Forms of Failure

On the other hand, some people fail to succeed in literature purely because they are terrible writers. That is not off the table yet, by no means. First of all, what is to be said by terrible writing? Boring, monotonous or even uninteresting. These are all factors, but it is only in the eye of the beholder that what is to be said as good is good and what is bad and what is bad. As said before, most books get pushed because they are written well: this is the general public's idea of "well written". And so, profiting businesses must take the general public's idea as they are the majority and so wish to be sold more.

There are, as in anything, too high expectations of which people have on their work. This is also a result of publicised pushing in action. As the reader, and soon-to-be-published author, will only see books that are being published and hearing of interviews of the pushed book's writer, they will believe, however, idiotic this may sound, that all, or at least the majority, of published books, will be pushed and that writing the manuscript is the hard part. What they fail to realise is that there are millions of other books which go unrecognised for every hundred or so that get pushed as Profit-Books.

The high expectations of what this person believes to be in the world of publishing are false, idiotic and benign. In comparison, the highest custom of an individual seeking readiness for publication is that they understand, appreciate and will learn to tolerate the pain, toil and hard work that must indefinitely come with the task.

One will quickly come to realise when reading that the art form of writing has sadly been taken mostly for granted in the modern age. For it is these people who will wreak the rewards for their down-to-earth and grounded thinking on the plane and sphere of logical thinking. There are many factors though as one cannot state what is truly bad or what is good as that all depends on the genre at hand and who it is that has been placed at the head of finding out whether it is well written or not. How is the person defined that will undergo the task of finding out whether it is well written or not? That I cannot say at this present moment as that all depends on a committee and is usually picked out by a person taking an exam to figure out their cognitive abilities and how well they can digest and dissect certain phrases: this person I am not. Instead, I can give in this essay what I am coining as the term Educated Assumptions in Terms of Advice. Stating that though I cannot call myself someone who can understand certain texts fully, as that would be self-centered and narcissistic, I instead leave that term to be given to me by the public consensus as in the example of choosing the person.

A person can drive a car, but whether they are a well-rounded and careful driver, is up to the general public and their passengers. So is the notion of a well-established author given to them by the general public and academic readers.

To publish this essay without mentioning failure in its true form is to be hypocritical of my own words previously. Failure, in this context, is to call it merely not reaching the level of what one was expecting in the eyes of one more successful predecessor. Even a few book sales are an achievement, and an unpublished, finished, manuscript is also by no means a failure. They all hold their meanings for what they hold in as that a man who has trained but not ever completed a marathon has not failed but succeeded in his moral rights.

The concept of publication and rejection from general and social persons must be factored in as inevitable or the writer is deemed naive and dangerous to their dispositions by all means necessary. Knowing what is reasonable about your potential can be the only way to succeed as potential is only as large as the person creating it is. If that is to say that they underappreciate themselves and undersell themselves, some more sales are seen in higher success rates of personal development. If the person is to oversell themselves, knowing the essay was lackluster, then they are to see themselves as failures of themselves rather than the true stance in failures of their mental selves.

One can believe in underselling themselves as to wish to gain higher profits, but this will fall into the category of Profit-Book making and that will subsequently lead to lackluster written pieces and the decrease in sales will be met with anything from anger to abuse (both self and others) instead of the aforementioned result of underselling; as in this case, the exhibiting person has undersold themselves and tricked their mind into believing something it cannot understand as it does not, deeply, believe it to be the truth. This is the fatal flaw of the mental perception: man cannot tell himself to love something he carries as mental din and vice versa.

CHAPTER 7
Classification of Failure

One cannot strictly tell if a piece is terrible as this is up to the eye and mind of the beholder. I like the work of Dickens, but my friend does not. She enjoys romance, but I do not. To state once again, man cannot deny himself what he believes and agree with what he disbelieves. I am, as a writer and individual reader, in no position or stance to call what is right or is wrong in an absolute sense in literature for the common man. The only advice I can give to him is on what *I* believe to be right or wrong. But I am in a stance as the general public and a member of the literary intelligentsia of the twenty-first century, to point out when a book, essay or piece is written correctly and has solely been made to profit man's intelligence and furtherment of the human race of which is more vital than money.

The context of "terrible" in this version can mean a range of things from that it is imperfect and has very few blemishes but overall is well-written, all the way to the other end of it seems to have been written by a man of very little intellect or school education in ten seconds. This is the scale. If I permit you to remember and recall the previous scene of electing the person best fit for the job of testing on what is good or not, then this is the perfect time to recall that as it seems to be the person reading it deciding whether it is terrible or not and that is the key difference. If your friend of many years was reading your pages, then they may be less critical of it in the hope of benefiting their friendship with the other person. Give it to a fully established writer and they will always hate it for two reasons: if it is written poorly, then they will dislike you and it for wasting their time. If it is well written, then they will dislike it for being better than their own and will envy you for the same reason previously justified.

It is crucial to never hand a piece of work to anyone of kin or friendship for evaluation as this will only result in the outcome of bias or anger. It is in this that the advice given is to give it only to a professional with no previous bias against you and no record of the author, to begin with. It is from this that they will create their evaluations and as they are the professional who marks and edits for a living, instead of writing, they will come out with true and crucial advice on what needs to be done to the piece to make it its best. This is the tale of ignorance to scholars.

There is a spectrum that follows in use with this gratification of an essay or piece and that is the spectrum of ignorance. The spectrum of ignorance is the application of the mental structure to honestly evaluate a piece or essay written by oneself. A spectrum such as this one is needed to have much meditation on the process of revising the evaluated sense. One cannot simply graze over their indulgences and seek it to be one of the best, though it is to be said that it could rightly become such but must seek their own mental companies and envisage it as a piece that must be criticized and critiqued within an inch of its lift. The meditation is to take place over many hours and even days or weeks or even months before one can conclude where in the spectrum their piece falls in line with other pieces written around the same time or the same length and the same volatile language. All these factors and more must come into play when figuring out where in the spectrum one's piece will fall with absolute certainty of unbiased decisions and no outside context which could hinder narcissistic beliefs.

One cannot stress enough how much the meditation process of the decision of the spectrum must take many months to configure as one is only able to speak to oneself if one is completely at peace and solemnity in one's mind, soul and body. For man is only what he sees in a mental mirror broken, the truth is shown clearer than any mirror before it.

It shines a light on the world around us, our complications and ourselves: this is the pure essence of writing.

In part of what is to be mentioned as content and solemnity in one's mind of what they have created, the writer must be seen from outside perspectives of their own eyes. Though this is not to be said for all writers, the ones who start and end, with the clearest values of self-loathing turn out to be some of the best as they have underappreciated their works. And the opposite will stand true, in most cases, for the majority of narcissistic writers. Often ending in anger or abuse.

Profit Booking sees this decline in the human mentality as a result of that it is a parasite on the mind. One cannot live without the other. With so much of a great amount of passing time between starting a piece and finishing it, there is plenty of time to imagine the fame and wonders that would occur when published. This is the parasite. If indoctrinated, the parasite will grow and engulf the human capacity leaving little left of a sphere of rational thinking.

If the document is to be doctored at the start, in turn lowering and grounding the expectations of oneself to a realistic goal, then the parasites will have nothing to feed on and the one subject will have free reign to continue with their toil without the ruin and spoil of the parasite changing how it is written.

CHAPTER 8
Obedient Readers

People, primarily students of literature, will only read a book either because they were told to because they are obliged to, or because somebody or something recommended them to read it. Not only will this diminish the value by which the book is read, but it leaves out the possibility of other possibilities of reading. The student, by no fault of their own, has always been told binary answers: do and don't; right and wrong, and either is or is not. The reader will undoubtedly be left without self-thought and consciousness and be scared to pick up any book that wasn't approved by their curriculum. This pushes the classist behaviour seen in the first few paragraphs where the strong and powerful books/ essays are pushed but the news is never given a second thought.

One of the main factors in this lack of reading from the sphere of cultural normality is fear or a lack of identity. People have spent most of their lives under the reign of the education system and know no other life than to follow orders and to read and understand what they are told to understand and pump out essays all in the same format and achieve the highest grades imaginable no matter what the cost. This fear will cause people to never want to leave the bubbles of their reasoning for the inane fear that it may be wrong or deemed unworthy of their time. For what, if any action made by man or the people and actions around him could ever be considered wrong with the act of reading for the intrigue and knowledge of man for further generations and the generational years in one's own life?

There is but one way to truly become free of this reign and that is to indulge in self-preservative reading. Reading for one's pleasure. This can be a curve that is hard to navigate as even parents constantly telling their children to read more is seen as an order and will, of course, break the free spirit from want. But if navigated correctly this curve of intellect will become the cornerstone of every child's reading and further education.

People, I exclude just children from this part for a couple of reasons: firstly, it is not just them who are tentative about learning now. This essay is directed at children but the more experienced readers with many years of experience in the philosophical texts of the past.

People who are in education have often looked at writing and reading as the core of it has to be done rather than it gets to be done. To begin to diminish this flame and relight a new one in its place, we must begin to understand that an essay is merely written as an attempt to convey information. This piece you read is written as an essay for I can never believe in any form of afterlife that the occupant of these pages will ever fully understand what I mean in these texts for my verse of coy tells me that it is never finalised and complete. But also, for that, the reader would require sitting with me for many years, too many to count, to fully talk extensively on this topic and sort it around so that it is complete and without the holes in the knowledge it originated from in its first draft.

To begin the diminishing of the flame it has to be said for the obvious that the human mind requires its ideas and its ideas only. It is from that that the choice of free expression can come into play. The student is told merely to write and never told why. The student is also told, for want of a better word: stupidly, that the text they must read is already told in their fortunes and will be seen in the essay. The text will have been told over and over again to the students of the past years. Therefore, it is very easy for many of the prior students to merely pass down this knowledge and intellect making it easier for the students of the present to pass the test.

But, in the same way, that a painter's emotions

come out on the canvas whether he likes it or not, the tone of the essay will convey the same. If the text is to be taught as boring and to be revised as dull and commonplace, then it will be written in such a fashion; that each student tells the same lines and the same metaphors in their essays. This form of teaching is mostly done to make it easy for the invigilators and people marking the exams, but it comes at the price of the imagination and free spirit of the writer, the student.

The student must be able to choose their texts to complete because, though this will make it harder for the marker to correct their errors and make sure of what is in the book or not, it will be to the benefit of the student and the to-be master of the craft to society. And that is what writing is, man's gift to society. If a man is without choice and reason, then we are doomed to repeat history forever.

When in past times, and the Soviet Union was still in operation, it saw the opening and subsequent closing of an iron curtain primarily built of books. Books, you see, are the force by which every great nation is driven. They are not pages of tales but pages and lives entwined in casings preserved for hundreds of years. If one is to control the flow of literature, then one controls the people.

The Soviet Union controlled its media tightly and

with iron fists. Only what was regulated could emanate from the cracks. Imagine a funnel of typewriters and at each one is a man, each stricter than the last. As the news is written, he passes it to the gentleman beneath him, he edits it and takes out the parts he believes to be blasphemous and the parts he believes to be changed: he changes. It is here that the earlier man must pay his price and is subsequently shot and replaced by a man of identical stature. As the page passes down this tower of regulation, the page is stricken and tarnished and by the time it has reached the base, there is but nothing left of the original, but a completely different story composed of the leader's wishes. This was the Union that so many depended on.

With travel outside of the country near to impossible for many reasons, money and education being a few of them, the people of the Soviet Union were dependent on the newspapers and the books they read (that is if they could read).

The one who controls the literature controls the people.

Briefly, there were no regulations to state that the writer had to have any credit, and the piece could be changed in the process of editing. The government could change what they wished to for their gain, and they could kill if the story was anti-Soviet. The government could, and would, carry the right to republication in other languages and the author may never need to know.

Alexi Pajitnov faced the same problem when he developed his famous video game "Tetris".

As time went on these rules would become more and more strict. The people would face this regime until 1973 when the regulations would become loose and more available. Authors were given their rights back and the government, though still playing a role in publication and copyright, rules became more relaxed as well.

This was until 1971 when there were rules set in place to make the Russian empire more closed off and turn back to the "Sustainable Soviet ideals" of the past. Fortunately, the Soviet Union dissolved before this could ever take effect. But for the practices of jest, imagine what life would be like for the Soviet people if the rule were passed and there were to be tighter regulations.

For he who controls the literature is to control the people.

It was during this time that the people of Russia depended on the Eastern ideas of literature and Television and had no connection to the outside world, or very little. In this little bubble, it came that people were still believing certain countries existed that had since dissolved after World War Two.

It is when the top per cent of people in a nation are

controlling, and I know I'm starting to sound a bit like a broken record, the literature and the media are effectively controlling the ones who indulge in it. A modern example of this would be that of the state of North Korea; or our own countries, wherever that may be for the reader, as we may never truly know how "Honest" our own countries are and in what medium the lies have been extended to fit their ideas. For all, we know we could be the bad guys.

And this should be taken as a warning to all that the literary intelligentsia are the most dangerous people on the face of the earth or if you can read and write effectively, that is a war on whomever it is to come across. Read the unread, write the unwritten and sing the unsung: for only then may man fight up and know the true meaning of freedom. When he is to find freedom in himself, he is to find freedom in life and accordance with the liberty of parochial office. Freedom of man is to be held sacred. Not freedom as free choice, freedom as it is the free choice to wake up, hours worked, and never need worry, or very little concern, on where the next meal is to come. (I understand, of course, that the last part is to sound uncultured and formatted as the light of the current crisis sees no sign of these fusions coming to pass, but humanity is nothing without something to aim for. A pre-mortem wish)

CHAPTER 9
Revolution to Obedience

To encourage this type of reading of smaller publications; schools, libraries and households should start employing a system of choosing a particular book to write an essay about and/or employing self-reading times in the morning and afternoon. Those who control the books, also control the minds of the young and naive. It is only by allowing the liberation of small media that the individual can become mass and have his/ her (or whichever socially acceptable version it is) voice or ideas heard.

Reading in this specific format is crucial for young and developing minds as it is non-binary thinking. Non-binary thinking is a format simply stating that the thought that a person or thing has undergone has been irrational, sporadic and uncaused by any force of the world around them: it is neither or either, is or is not, left or right, or do and don't. The choice a person or thing made to choose that piece of literature and read that piece alone, was their own doing: not hindered by recommendations, forced educational reading, or peer pressure on trending. Purely their own choice.

If the person can undergo their own choices in reading then they can explore this new-found liberty in whichever manner they choose. They can choose to read and write about pieces that have since gone unnoticed because of the sheer, stupidly ignorant, fact of uninterest in the schooling board. Or deemed too modern.

The student will realise that he wishes to read the piece ascribed to him, as it was his own choice in the matter, but also because he feels independent. The piece he will produce will be written vibrantly and, in a style, befitting him. This is the problem and solution I present to the education board. Listen to my warning, heed it or face the consequence of faceless, mindless and intellectually challenged human-like drones: prostitutes to society and the nine-to-five.

There is, as in anything, a cure for such reading dissolutions. And that is simply to explore. For if humanity is without its gathering nature, it has nothing. Humans, homo sapiens to be exact, have always been the hunters in the ecosystem. This leads us in the modern age to hunt for consumerism. The boredom of the human mind completes, or at least believes it completes itself, by buying things and trinkets. It is in this net that the human mind is to fall. A proverbial spider web if you will.

The mind will search for its next catch, but this is hard to find, and the human mind is lazy, therefore it looks to others who claim to know all and what is good to purchase, hunt, and their next trophy.

These 'people' are the ones who are the marketers. They will be the gods that power the media and pressure them into the purchase. From this, the profit book has gained more traction with mindless consciousness, and the common book has been left to defend itself in the corners of the media: print or digital.

There are, as always, ways to break this habit and that can follow in the simple sense of, reading the unread. Look out for the small books in the corners of the media and on small advertisements and those are the ones that shall be the ones you read.

This method of reading tried and tested by myself will firstly allow the reader to gain an understanding of what they truly love in their mind, not what they merely trick themselves into believing.

Secondly, there is an understanding of what literature and ideas are. Most Profit-book writers claim in interviews, that the social construct they feed on, understand what they write and tell of it having deep and misunderstood readings and lessons: this is not true.

From my own experiences, in cafes I shall not tell the name of, I have been caught in conversation with many individuals who claim to have written original ideas, first arrogant and incorrect, and then who further claim to have written dark and deep meanings into their pieces. This is also not true, for want of a better word, as the idea they so crave was thought up in a matter of seconds when their only two neurons intertwined for the first time in a blue moon and also because the statement is almost always followed up with the question: "So, how much did you make when you got published?"

When reading there is the imperative stature to read the unread the write the unwritten. The greatest honour a writer can inherit is having their book banned. If there are to be Profit Books, it is a lot like drugs: never rid of, but reduced in amount, then they are to be at least tolerated ones and not ones purely written for money and ones that at least have some credibility in the field of the intelligentsia. For it is these behemoths of ideocracy who shape the word of the common man to mold the minds of the outside man into seeing our works as evil and dull and commonplace while making theirs seem amazing and once in a century.

BOOK III

CHAPTER 10
Liberty Including Free Will

The common reader as well as the writer must also be allowed to read what they desire. An elephant who is tied up will only venture as far as its imaginary rope once removed from the tether. The same is said for people. When only told what they can read, in school that being classics and approved literature, once removed from the setting; they have no prior experience in anything else and therefore will eternally believe that reading anything other than the classics, or socially popular fantasy, is wrong by the highest degrees of reading.

There is, as in most things, the scientific reasoning behind the fact reading is for one's pleasure. The main point of a Profit Book is to ensure the reader or buyer a chance to never think about what they read or what it is they wish to read about. Being placed at the forefront of a shop, the Profit Book entices with, normally pastel, colours and minimalist covers. The buyer is to be thinking that they have heard of this book on some sort of media and that it should now be bought and then read whilst also posting pictures of themselves reading the book, also known as free advertisement and higher pushing for the Profit Book and less bought for the new publisher.

The reasoning lies in that the comprehension of self-indulgence of the mind in what one likes is proving to reproduce higher levels of brain activity and the bonus of brain growth. When a person buys and reads a book for their indulgence without a second thought on what the outer world is to believe, then they are to be classified as an intellectual individual. This Intellectual Individual can be seen as an individual by taking their stance and, literally, not judging a book by its cover. This person will seek rewards and gain those rewards on cranium indulgence and cognitive thought. They will read whatever is necessary for them at the present moment and indulge in it completely until they are fulfilled: even if this means having to take themselves to the corners of a library and seek out dusty pamphlets and books for the information they seek.

This indulgence can also be said for the individual

who reads as a mere relaxing factor. Though there is less beauty and point to this method than I would like, it is still one of worthy mention and one that, when done correctly, will produce storytellers unknown to the common man at this specific point in time and space.

If the individual is without common thought and lacks the capability of self-knowledge on what one truly wishes, then they are without success and submit themselves to the layers of damnation and ideocracy known as a mindless automaton. Following automotive actions under the pretense that they see themselves as free will students and their options and opinions are unequaled and individual, but they are mere slaves to mindless automation.

There is, as many other intellects would state, a benefit to reading and indulging one in one's craft of choice. If the person is to only read profit books, then they are to reproduce the same errors in humanity's evolution. But, if they are to break free from the chains of bounded reading, they can become the best writers known. It is with this that comes benefits of magnitude in the inclusion of writing better.

When focused solely on the benefit of the craft for oneself and the betterment of humanity, the person is to succeed. If the person indulges in a meaningless discourse of literature and is solely focused on the betterment of credentials, status and monetary benefits, they are to seek these benefits but break the contract signing themselves to any form of self-liberty and become literary prostitutes.

For if a man has nothing but his liberty, then he is freer than the one who sold himself for quick fame.

CHAPTER 11
Classifications of Failure

When people are being told what they can and cannot read about, this will affect what they believe they can think and write about. This is due to that they have been informed, and so have been informed to believe, that this one-in-a-thousand book is to be the ordinary and universally set standard. In another essay, I have spoken about why this is deceitful to young minds and how a filtered and rendered version of the publication will be detrimental to the general writer. The writer, being a free spirit, must be allowed to conceive their imagination in whichever way they wish to: given that they are not harming others physically or detrimentally psychologically in the process of doing so. If, as George Orwell phrased it, people were to sell their literary intellect to the media and only write what the heads want them to write; they would in turn become literary prostitutes. It is one of the last truly individual art forms left.

In a turn of effect, this shall cause the person, we'll call them person A for now, the writer, to gain an air of lacking comfort in the face of the publication. And as they wish to publish their works, they must also find a publisher. With the lack of confidence in publication backing their minds, they will set themselves up for failure in this presence. Person A sends off many pieces to many publishing houses and receives them back all declined. There are many factors which could cause such a thing to happen, and the main one is that Person A's piece was purely not interesting or written poorly. But the other reason which I wish to stress from the multitude of others is that in the publishing house, there is to be narrowed down to two competitors for their piece in a let's say a literary review (we'll call this Act B)

From these two there is only one spot left inside Act B for a piece to go. As the manager of Act B only makes a profit on the capital of the consumer-free market, he must make his paper as intriguing as possible. I will not dare to bore you with the linguistics and basics of any marketing strategy for any amount of time longer than I have, so if there is to be one spot and two competitors for that spot: Person A and C, and it turns out that person C is famous as a movie star but the piece was written very unflavoured and bland, nine times out of ten the manager of Act B will choose Person C as for their parochial office and name for the cover, but very rarely the newly-upcoming person A, as this would add nothing to the minimal profit margins the company of Act B are already making.

This, in turn with the last statement, can and will deter the students and new writers from publishing or even writing their books. This is the cause of the combined evil of the mental structures introduced and enforced in schools and higher education, and sometimes even in parental guidance methods: though this is rare.

When the writer is learning the skill they do so of their mentality and their curiosity about the methods. The Profit Books are to place an immediate end to this curiosity stream.

These Profit Books, written as stated by celebrities and people of high importance or just written by a perfectly placed algorithm to turn out the highest profits, these books are to deter the learner from wanting to publish because what is the point of swimming uphill when the food is all gone? In this analogy, the Profit Book writers have already been given a helping hand in publishing and wreak the rewards when the little fish, the newly published person, must fight upstream and life and death, only to find out that their reward is nought and that there is not to be any for them. The fat fish grins.

When newly published or about to publish people see this they are put off and ever even want to consider the possibilities of getting their book out there; as it is a gamble and highly risky. With thousands of books being published every day, whether that be self or traditional, the market is too competitive. Books are less expensive to buy and make than what they were, let's say, a thousand years ago, but there is still that cost. Self-published authors take on the added misfortune of having to do all their marketing, but there is the glorious bonus of, depending on where you go, being able to single print where the person will only pay for what is to be ordered. In traditional publishing there is a bigger risk as the individual will pay for the books to be printed in bulk, this is more for first-time authors and those not returning, this starting price can be anywhere from two to four thousand pounds and that is not guaranteeing that they are all to be sold. That is to be left to the marketing department.

But the second question that can be asked in the eyes of publications is why people will continue to write in the face of a wall in front of them and the chances of successful publications having odds set against them. I wish to add that there is to be some gratitude and not complete Nihilism on my behalf. Because, although I do believe that there is very little to no good in the world with people never getting a starting chance and the media being leeches on the carcass of the common man; I do not wish to in any way discourage the common reader and writer.

When writing there are to be risks with all, and a writer should only compete if willing. Such as you would not spend a lifetime competing in races if it were not enjoyable or a career opportunity. The same is to be said for writing. If there is to be a faint glimmer, then there is to be a faint glimmer shining upon the page of the paper that covers their manuscript. But that gamble is up to the individual and their social circumstances. Great works are often thought of in the corner shops and bus stop benches. But it is also needed that the story be beholden of a learned mind to carry the weight and burden of writing such a piece. The ordinary, conformity mind is unable to do this; though it is the same story.

This edit and detour of the daggers in publishing have taken the focus off from the main course of

Profit Books, so I wish to return to that. When there are Profit Books to be sold, more of the focus and the Profit Book. There will, of course, be a focus placed on the selling of the non-profit book, but less so.

The other note I wish to add is that there is to be decided by the large public on what is a Profit Book. This is not to state that for it to be a Profit Book the writer must be pure and never once think of making any money. Every writer must think of money at some point in their time writing, or what is it all for and how will they pay the bills? But a Profit Book is to be stated as one that has been written, divided and made by a mental algorithm to incorporate the highest strength of profit there is to make. The characters are chosen, ethnicity and lifestyle, to incorporate this. The scenes and language are chosen to incorporate these as well. Written fast, edited once (or not at all) and published. I also speak of the small writer, the person reading this may think that of themselves and place themselves into the mental mind space of this small writer. Though this is true, that is not to state that the small writer is not a Profit Book Writer. It may be that the person reading this essay is a Profit Book Writer and is too naive to figure out such a title. But that will become apparent from when it is published and then the public leaves their reviews. A person cannot decide whether they are a good writer, the general public does.

The best thing a person can do for themselves in writing is to reach maturity on realising that they are to be self-recognised as Profit Writers, aesthetic writers, or procrastinators. Because self-acceptance and realisation is the first step in breaking habits.

When a person or writer is to understand themselves as such that is not to say they should change, it is to say what they should publish. When a profit book writer realises that they are such and permits themselves to the hand of change, then they are to succeed as they have realised how writing is meant for the betterment of people and humanity. Whether that be a story for young children to increase their grammar capabilities, for young adults to teach them about sex, or for philosophers to teach them about life and death.

When there is a writer who realises and regards the notion of their changing as a mere waste of a life's accomplishments, then they are to fail. Also, if the writer reads their books and wishes not to change themselves, they are to be classified as arrogant by their back-most mind and the intellects around them. If the arrogant writer falls into denial, saying that there is nothing wrong with their piece and looks closely for any little thing that they can call Non-Profit: language, ideals, lifestyle etc., then they are to be made fools and always Profit Writers.

Writers should go into their pieces with clarity on what they wish to achieve with the piece and how they wish to execute it. If that spark is not there then it is doomed to fail and they will always be literary prostitutes - a title coined by George Orwell to classify people who sell their proverbial souls to the public and write only what the public wants. Seeling a soul for a bit of money, thus; literary prostitutes.

CHAPTER 12
Rejection of Advice and Reason

If the individual is to throw out all means of recognition and reject everything, he will eventually mistake himself for God and believe that he can create his reality. But, cut out from the rest of his society, he will produce nothing but words on a page.

There is nothing to show for his isolation and, though a thrilling experience, there is nothing to resemble the enticing and profound use of vocabulary which is associated with well-written literature. To claim what is written as truth and glorious work, one must pass it and evaluate it by peer recommendation. Not through the peers of close relatives and friends, but peers of professional standard who will give harsh truths to the piece and commentate it is well written. The well-evaluated person of which is to oversees the making, editing and eventual publication is to be a person with a respected career behind them who published many of their books that have been well acclaimed under these laws of Recognition and publicity and not the laws on the publicity of multiple Profit Books. The person seeking is making a mock-innocent fool of themselves if the editor they hire is to tell them comforting lies. One cannot lie to oneself if what they are to complete is published through nepotism or popularity.

There are exceptions to the rule of "Nobody shut off from the world". But they must take into account the principles of Emil M. Cioran to test if they are the exception. The principles are that of failure and they will govern life whether they are well or not. If one is to surround themselves with the failures of their own life, then they are to see the errors and change them to make better of their work. If one is to never look at these errors in a true sense, then they are to fall into the trap of forever repeating themselves in these errors.

CHAPTER 13
Idealistic Writing

Recognition is to state that the individual or group is recognised by the leading party as one of them and will create work just the same as that which is expected in the field. Many times, though the recognition can be because of that which is Profit Booking. The recognition sold and acclaimed here is the other type and that is the inconclusive way of recognising literary works. The notion of freedom of the press comes to mind when talking about the recognition in the modern age, and it is most informed that when talking about propaganda publications the mind races to the authoritarian ruling countries such as North Korea, Kazakhstan and Soviet Russia. And the notion of freedom of speech is thought of when talking about democracy and Western worlds such as the United Kingdom and the United States of America.

When there is to be propaganda and the use of authoritarian force there will be the liquidation and control of the media and especially literature. For many, this is to say that all, or most, major and sub-major publications are to accept a majority of pieces submitted lest they be sullen and labelled as the authoritarian publication party. But the people of these Western worlds must understand the true impact of literature on the common man. If the publication were to publish every piece without thought of the consequences of their actions, then it could most primarily descend the countries into chaos. For, if every action is to have consequences, then each party, singular or company, must choose the path more calming to the unknown future.

The publication must choose the pieces to publish depending on three things:

1: It has comprehensive mental applications for the reader.

The book will succeed and only succeed if the reader is to learn from it. For the man is not a complete man if he is not learned from his time. A book, by definition, is intended for the reader to learn whether that be philosophy, literature, drama or any other, smaller, subjects including the ability to spell, write or calculate arithmetic. These are the pillars the book is built.

Let us state though that Profit Books can create the need for mental intuition after it has been read, one should be able to evaluate the necessity and worth of the intuition as their verdict on whether or not it was a Profit Book or not.

It is these clear and honest insights of oneself that can distinguish the premises given and the laws stated observed what is and what isn't worth the time or effort of the intellectual.

2: The Book shall be as long as it is and nothing more or less.

When the individual is writing it is imperative fact that the essay, book or article is not restrained by minimum or maximum word counts but be liberated at what the length is in its whole. The moment a piece has any sort of unmitigated paragraphs or chapters that have the reader uninspired or interrupt the flow of language, it results from itself to now be condemned by the bounds and laws of Profit Books.

It is the responsibility of the author to understand the wheat from the chaff in their work. If the piece is to end up at one hundred pages, then it shall be that and understand itself holding itself by its own merits.

3: It will benefit only the reader and the parties it is intended for.

Whereas the Profit Book has the misguided intuition of incorporating as many parties as possible and as many individuals to it, the Non-Profit-Book understands its worth by its own merits and directs itself towards the parties and individuals it is intended for and nothing more. The language written will be understood by the parties or individuals and they only save for the exception of curious outsiders who seek better understanding upon their own free will.

Once learned enough to understand each of its limitations, failings and the principles all respective books must follow to be understood and held high, then they are free to write their works.

CHAPTER 14
Rogues in Writing

One must probably walk down many streets before you can call them a man and yet it is never explained or vocalised that someone must walk down many altercations and evaluate many choices before you can call them learned. Few people can call themselves learned in the fields of literary and higher learning, but many people will call themselves learned: these are the fake literary icons or literary prostitutes.

And it is in the interest of the Profit Booking mind to seek great rewards without putting in any major or critical work.

England, the Americas and a majority of the Western world have seen this as an uprising in the last thirty years. And, as it is as previously stated, in the best interest of the publisher to profit off their sold works. As a rule, profit is the key to staying stable in life and keeping the economy up. But when sacred and great arts such as literature become sullied by the names of greed and lust, then it is to be desired and forwarded that the protocols and verses be under stricter sanctions for the mainstream.

Creative liberties are the humanitarian sanctions all great and poor men and women are gifted at birth, and it dictates whether we are human or not. The higher sanctions though should be set in place when the majority of books become Profit Books by their very nature of existing.

In a perfect world of meaninglessness, and a universe centered on sporadic consequences, a literary rogue, a friend of the literary prostitute, will seek reward from the calamity, further himself, and focus his mind and energy on easy profit. A literary mind such as The Rogues is to show no danger in the adversity of danger when writing or publishing. He and the Profit Publications are on the same proverbial pages when it comes to publishing and that is categorised under the mere act and intention of profiting under the ratio of minimal work done to the greatest rewards given. Enduring this behaviour in the writer is dangerous and he will begin to seek higher rewards. The nature of the universe being absurd alongside the person of such a rogue and brash nature is an imperative justification focusing on the adversity of moral and ethical behaviours.

Regarding back to the notion that all actions must

have consequences, religious or not, it is followed that certain individuals do not see the need to follow these rules. Eventually, while playing the long game and playing facade to the facts around them, the future literary worlds will become sullied not for their images and representation, but for past idiotic pieces sullying the name of what is not yet even in existence.

Yet it is to be exclaimed that each piece stands by its own merits, the human and her common brethren see it as a whole and demise the individual for showing credibility and integrity when faced with diversity and individuality. In excruciating circumstances, the rogue will be caught with their words and punished by whatever means are necessary for such an act. However, individuals need to educate themselves on what is and what is not profit. This is the word of an intellect and an absurdist who claims no right to tell what is and what is not. But continue to read this, so the reader has an understanding of what it means when I state these concepts.

CHAPTER 15
The Varied Intellectuals

Such a basis of understanding what is and what is not Profit Booking requires extreme knowledge and recollection from many varied viewpoints on what is classified and labelled as well written and informants on the characteristics of Non-Profit Books and working towards the end goal of betterment for mankind. One must intentionally and tragically come to the understanding that the Profit Booking is not truly and wholly up to the publisher who is responsible for printing, but every man, woman and child also has to understand and protest against this. The third is the Rogue, the one responsible for writing the piece and this is the worst of the parties involved as they carry the grief and understanding, or more often than not the lack of such, of what they have done: even if they do not express it publicly. If they fail to understand this and take the necessary actions against themselves, then they have failed mankind. If they are to understand and neglect their thoughts in pursuit of betterment for themselves, then they have foregone any and every right mental and physical that classifies them as human by state or individual liberty. Every man must find these injustices and state them as a hindrance to the creative freedoms of others.

It is also the job of every reader to teach themselves and be sufficiently in the direct line or equal line mentally on understanding education and the contrary beliefs of what is in Profit Books. For this to be understood, one must learn what it means to be an academic intellectual.

Even I at points in this essay have questioned my ability the understand what is considered an existence of academic intellect. It would be impossible to talk about said relations without first justifying what an academic is and what an academic piece of work is.

The young, a person under 21 in this scenario, often consider themselves intellectuals by seeing themselves cornered off and so, logically, without anyone to call them wrong but also having a naive mind, they will call themselves genius. But it is the modern academic we focus on here. If I were to take a traditional academic, I would classify them as a phenomenology centered around a dark bubble of further learning. Reading always for better understanding and compromising books from a variety of sources as to exile bias and include further understanding. The Modern academic is quite the same in that they also strive for higher learning, though they focus more on one primary topic to write, paint or talk about and act more like dictators upon themselves rather than intellectuals, though calling them anything other than an intellectual: Absurdist, Marxist, Nihilist; but while never actually expressing any views or behaviours on the parties they supposedly follow. Ours is an age where there are fewer and fewer true intellectuals. The majority of self-diagnosed intellectuals resemble more a group of naive children with a better understanding of the world; though lacking any way to communicate with it.

Heading onwards it is necessary to define and solidify the understanding of an academic paper or book. An academic paper or book that aims to teach certain levels and values. Numbers, spelling, arithmetic, and succeeding one another up until it reaches higher education. However, this differs from a philosophical book as the academic book does not question circumstances in such a manner. Instead, it questions things in a simplified manner that does not try to explain the higher questions such as the sanctity of our meaning in life.

To be understood under the terming of modern academics is to seek out higher knowledge, read and learn from varied sources and write as well as discuss with many different characteristics. Ludwig Wittgenstein said in his 1922 book Tractatus Logico-philosophicus

"The limits of my language mean the limits of my world."

It would be foolish to state and assume that all Profit Books are merely a manifestation of a naive intellectual with an impudent mind. Rather we, the intellectuals, should see those authors by their own merits regarding their philosophies and understanding of the topic and hold the unanimous agreement of what is and if not a Profit Book. And the apathy in modern culture on praising every task to the gravitas of genius on greatness is only certain to sully and foolishly deny the facts of life being an eccentric amalgamation of conquerors and failures.

At this point, I perceive and recall a final statement. There must be a commonly held conception that there are two states of understanding when it comes to writing. One must consider the two states to be mentioned as separate entities in the mind of the intellectual. Firstly, there is love. The anguished awareness of love for aesthetical purposes but also the sheer uniformity and comfort it brings. This person may write for themselves, though whether or not it should be published by self-means or traditional is to be left to the general public and the aforementioned literary intellectuals to consider whether they are a well-informed and valuable asset to writers or not. The question is, why or how does a writer for mere love understand whether they are a Profit Book writer or not? This can and has been answered earlier in the essay. But it could also be found in the way it is presented and performed. It is also the duty of all literary intellectuals and the common man to understand and criticise justly whether it is or is not a Profit Book.

Secondly, there is the individual who completes these tasks under the influence of his love for them. The tasked and intellectual man strives for a better understanding of certain subjects and simultaneously shares them with mankind. The difference between the masked man and the follower of love is that the latter does not undertake the practice of publishing for publication's sake but publishes what is necessary. He recognises his struggle and submits to enjoyment in his craft.

BOOK IV

CHAPTER 16
Education Regarding Crafts and Fools

The philosophers have seen these statements made and unanimously they agree some silently, some violently that it is the birth sovereignty of every man to withhold and keep sacred those such precious machines capable of wars, injustices and enlightenment for they are records of the human race as a whole piece. There are books and papers written that have ignited wars. Then there are the martyrs who write away the rubble. And finally, there is the hero who writes to ensure sanctity, embassy and silence from destruction.

If we as humans are to continue to call these Profit Books equal to the great liberation; then we have greatly failed. Though these injustices carry on. And in due to fair justice, I will carry out the third point containing what has been said as well as editing onto it a personal solution.

If it were up to me there would be a worldwide ban of all Profit Books and all books overseen by a mandate to control flow, but that goes against my own beliefs as well as the right of man for freedom of speech and creative liberty. Instead, it should be that the education system must change. Everyone strives for more and this is unjustifiable. However, the modern education system is flawed in that it teaches students that they are the best at what they do and try. This is most prevalent in American states and the rest of the Western world. And it is of surprise or genius throughout the United Kingdom or the United States of America that these children are not the best in their fields.

The education system in the United States of America and the United Kingdom should begin to gravitate towards understanding that the child can achieve greatness or mild success and that it will take many years of hard work and dedication to said craft of their choice. They must also be taught an existentialist truth the search that every human is born without meaning and that they must create meaning to it through education and many years of individual meditative thought. Contrary to that, the old way of teaching that everyone is born with purpose through fate should be taken away and replaced with existential thought experiments.

Understanding also the notion of failure is key.

Children, primarily from my age group, were all the ways told in school and colleges through assemblies that if you were to fail then you should try again and again. This motto is fine for school children as they are failing and experimenting then trying and again is the only way they can propose their grade to be better but in the adult world and literary Earth, it is a 50/50 progress. On the one hand, the writer cannot learn unless he revives his work and ethics and finds flaws in himself and the society that built him and changes them. also, the writer cannot write everything perfectly every time. Before he can call himself a writer, he must bind his voice and revise that. But to say that if he were together a floor rejection letters, he is to without failure, you must try many pieces. if he has written many pieces and all of them are against him, then he has discussed that either writing is not for him, or he must keep going. Either way, the majority consensus would say to him that this failure was due to him not producing anything worthwhile and that the only publishers that would take him were the Profit Publishers. So, he must decide; take what he has been given into the world as a failure when publishing what he rightfully knows is terrible or perceive onwards and keep going to where he wants. Or you can take the most common and frankly, right effort in the poor man's scenario and that is to hold his proverbial head high that might to himself and the world that's writing, as a schoolcraft, is not for him and move on to a new craft or carry on his love for writing and reading are they personal craft rather than a social one.

Education in all countries it's paramount to that cautious future. but it is not enough to merely state that actions must be undertaken to the core set, and as of now, the education system is on the edge of the cliff waiting to fall into a pit of failure. Action must be undergone to create maximum change.

The education system is flawed beyond the realm of renewal, but we can continue to live in a naive world. "The unexamined life is not worth living." Socrates stated in his essay" insert here" and precisely it is true. and though the profit booking industry is run by the state parties that own them, they are contributed to and fed by the unsophisticated writer. All of this behaviour begins in the academic classrooms.

Whether we will begin to exclude certain Media from the reach of the younger generations, much like the United Kingdom did with cigarettes from 2006 to 2007, the eradication of search materials should be undergone.

The entirety of the free, primarily Western, world agrees that the censorship of whole works goes against all included liberties regarding birth and said country, or expatriate citizenship in the national regions. And when the full understanding of the effects is learned can they begin to change the ethics to which they have previously condemned themselves.

CHAPTER 17
Profit Booking as a Publication

It is a tragic world we live in and yet we refuse to live tragically. and it is this tragic life we have those results in the blossoming of such books. The words which we write have meaning beyond what we know and will ever know as there is the self of the time we are living in the current sense. And then there is the self who is gone, the virtual self. They do know not what words come back as they do not know what trivialities the future holds with which they are here or are no longer. this is the absent mind that fills his mind with the now, which is concerned with living by but not for writing by. They will never think while their mind is active of the consequences and implications of their merciless words which are no longer there. A dissident mind is the deadliest as it cannot even know its implications.

And it is modern implications that cause the need and our society for modern revolts against oppression that has been sitting on the collective noses for generations. There is always to be an oppressor in realities unknown so there is even more need to evolve constantly as a liberty is for another than revolt in the destruction of collective means introduced by other parties with intentions for Think more of their product.

Though it is the sole duty of every man woman and child it says within the conflicts of revolt for means of liberation. That is to include the liberation of the arts, large and small, but the duties of latter learning of Profit Booking. Considering such profundities, the individual must grow themselves and create a literary world many are comfortable in and can learn from. And though the world has seen many books written for the pleasures and understandings and even the world we inhabit, there has been an uprising of literary works dedicated to mere profit and major thinking of the implications it may have down the proverbial line of human history.

The final is only enough when the Profit Booking scheme is bought a mere corpse lying down upon the embodied grave of what it once was. And it is through the education of the young, the old, and the new readers that the books catered towards such profound goals are reduced.

When, much like in the myth of Sisyphus, we are to not torture the author, but instead extinguish the action which the plume of Profit Booking came from. So we have them at the bottom of the Mountain. With the satisfaction of a downward rolling boulder is far too great a reward for which the misdeeds of the books have caused in the generations.

It is therefore no longer a question regarding the implications of the Profit Book in both present and future settings, but a question regarding the authenticity of the writer or whether their peace is profit or not. A related section begins by explaining the capacity and leeway an individual may place upon themselves to learn what a Profit Book is and how we can go about setting justice to an uncaring world. the opening of the mind that there will always be certain individuals who do not care for the notions of morality is key in understanding the act of options and extraordinary representation of such people and crafts. there seems to be an equal or slightly equal response when it comes to the discussion of free will and the same ratio when talking about absurdism. Imagining the two majorities, which we will call A and B respectfully, as singular people it becomes exponentially easier to imagine without crossed wires. And though the majority will include many different variations of the same type of person, the joint trails of the masses. Similarly, knowing he is free will and understanding his literary creativity is held by no bounds, he writes with this newfound freedom and calls it upon himself to reflect fully on his newly found capability and parts thought and care into all his works and works as to teach others about literary worlds and the meaning in his own. He will also consider before publishing whether he was true to himself and whether he's truly called with the nature of such he has put into this fold of paper. If all is well and up to code set by himself and his own volition, he will proceed to send it to be printed.

To think of the other side, the individual B, we must first undergo the understanding of therefore process. Firstly, they are educated in the literary arts, either self or traditionally, and they have written many pieces already: short stories, a few unpublished works and a novel of which they are thinking to publish. When they learn about the ethics of an existentialist belief and primary absurdism, they are found at a crossroads. Individual B can traverse the path of individual A, but knowing the latter path faces easier fame and more profit, he decides to navigate down the latter path.

It appears to be that after these brief descriptions, both individuals begin the same, sparky, young, and ever eager to write. But when faced with the same pros, they diverge paths one down one way and the other down another. And so, it strives to obtain the realisation as to why the two went down separate paths. It is far from thought now that the voluntary writer is to undergo a thought miraculous spell while writing that is to give them a 50/50 chance of being Profit or Nonprofit Writers. But none that the thought exercise of individuals A and B are the causes of human free will in an uncaring universe for stop both are proposed multiple paths, virtually more than what was mentioned. and they decide to, with their newfound free will, choose the correct path but then in their own free will and only them without passing a secondary thought for others for a stop that was the result of an individual mind. The first encounter with free consciousness is not enough to waver a mind, but the realization of the possibility will reside mentally forever where it was thought up.

The thought process is there also to demonstrate the crucial observation and that is to understand that Profit Booking is an individual decision and that though the learners' man can begin to eradicate such box, they may be diminished or shoved, the day will always be written by a select few who refused to expel them from their thoughts.

In the absurdist reality, I have explained that the liberty of free will be unguided by a set of rules is given by right to every man, woman and child and given at birth and that it is up to the individual to create their meaning to life with the question of God or any higher being involved. And that is speaking frankly, is the proposed that I set these regulations apart from the media, which may or may not be a fact, would be classified and may be seen as a representative of myself posing closure to certain liberties stated and then we'll go against my absurdist ethics. The difference between the ethics of someone's beliefs and the belief of someone's differences is the primary essence that condemns us from being humans.

Whether the individual is religious or not, we must understand the importance of morality. as acceptance that though individually man is free, the masses must obey the governing rules of the state or parties. Much like Meursault in Camus' "The Outsider". The everyday man must come to the dreaded realisation that, though while on his own time, you can do as he pleases rejecting the state laws that are placed there will grow upon you to be sentenced for humanitarian crimes. Meursault kills somebody on a beach to see what it feels like. though the methods of his actions and intentions were absurd, he condemns himself to be placed in prison for his action to stop the Profit Book writer is a lot like Meursault in that though their absurdist birthright gives them the freedom to carry out such tasks, the result of the actions to the rest of the world and the gravity of the failure of consequences, nobody in sense of any certainty aspect will cause an outcome much like Meursault. Except that the prison penalty is in this circumstance, unmitigated fame and harsh damage to the pillars of human literary creation. While the possibility of cheap and easy gratification may at first sound like a great thought and one that many wish to undertake, the consequences if not provoked onto self, are detrimentally harmful to the rest of the world.

Let us return to the start and that is the proposal on why people will continue to write Profit Book and what the consequences may be if the trend continues though the second point may not be aimed directly at its attention, it is the attention of all areas that must be demonstrated and brought to the attention of the mental image if the subject is to be understood as a whole idea past from one to the other without miscommunication.

CHAPTER 18
Writers and Their Works

It is therefore no longer a question regarding the implications of the Profit Book in both present and future settings, but a question regarding the authenticity of the writer or author that piece is profit or not. A related section earlier inspired explaining the capacity and Leeway an individual may place upon themselves to learn what a Profit Book is and how we can go about setting justice to an uncaring world. The opening in the mind that there will always be certain individuals who do not care for the notions of morality is key and understanding the rest of the set of options and the extraordinary representation of such people and crafts.

There seems to be an equal or slightly equal response either way when it comes to the discussion of free will and the same ratio when talking about absurdism. Inquiring about the two majorities, which we will call A and B, as singular people then need to become exponentially easier to imagine without cost wires. And though the majority will include many different variations of the same type of person, the singular is combined and made up from the joint traits of the masses. The singularity of knowing his free will and understanding that his literary creativity is held by no bounds. He writes with this newfound freedom causing himself to reflect fully on his newly found capability and put thought and care into all of his words and works to teach others about literary works and the meaning of his own. He will also consider before publishing whether he was true to himself and whether he is truly satisfied with the outcome of the work he has cut into this fold of paper. It all is well and up to a code set by himself and his own volition, he will proceed through sending it to be printed. To think of the other side, individual B, we must first undergo and understand their thought process first they are educated in the literary arts, either self or traditionally and they have written many previous pieces already. Short stories, a few unpublished novels, and many more. When they learn about the ethics of an absurdist belief and primary absurdism, they are based at a crossroads. individual B can either traverse the path of individual A, but knowing the first path faces easier fame and more profit, they decide to traverse down the latter path.

It appears to be that after this brief description, both individuals begin the same, sparky, young and eager writers, but when based on the same paths, they always diverge paths, one down the way of easy fame and the other the way of hard and honest work with a greater reward for the view who listen for stop and so it strives obtain realization why the two went down separate paths. It is from thoughts now that the voluntary writer is to undergo a sort of miraculous spell while writing it is to give them a 50/50 chance in the unconscious mind of either being Profit or Non-Profit Writers of books. But more than the thoughts exercised of individuals A and B are the causes of human free will in carry universe. both are proposed multiple paths, infinitely more than what was mentioned. They decide to, with their newfound free will, choose the path that will be correct for them in their own free will and mind and only without primary or secondary thought for others will stop that was the result of an individual mind. The first encounter with free consciousness it's not enough to relieve a mind, but the consistency of possibility will reside mentally forever where it was thought up.

An image defined and crafted by the individual mind is to be different for each person. eats choice of paths and new strokes on the canvas and through we all begin from no essence, the literary work ethical and metaphysical ethics

The thought process is they're also to demonstrate the crucial surge and that is to understand that Profit Booking is an individual craft and through the learner, man can begin to create such box, they may be minimized or shunned, but they will still always be written by such people who refuse to expel their thoughts.

CHAPTER 19
Non-Existent Best Sellers

In New York and many other cities across the globe for that matter, there has always been a fundamental agreement and coalition in mind that where there is a Profit Book Publisher, there needs to be an agreement with the general media to birth a Profit Book Reader. Much like how Henry Ford invented the manual assembly line, he also needed to create a workforce to maintain his machines and build his cars.

The thought alone that a workforce can survive without its most crucial of strengths: the people, is an absurd afterthought on the subjective literary, economic, and moral identities that the modern world is secluded inside of.

Intrinsically there are two types of society when it comes to the subject of the workforce and the Idol workforce. Firstly, what is the idle workforce? An idle workforce is comprised of and distinguished by being the secondary forces that govern the purchasing of the items; goods and services as well as the products they supply. Representation of this field is comprised of almost everyone due to the need for everyday goods: food, Entertainment and some not-so-necessary foodstuffs and trivialities. I say is most largely represented by humans and not all due to the idea of hermit and recluses which are the ideals of both workplaces. However, the primary workforce will fall into this scenario as they too are responsible for the purchasing of necessary and luxury items. And so the problem can be stated, seen and solved as such: the idea that workplaces can survive without any necessary forms of workforces, then the system is to fail and condemn itself to be nine and docile to its tactics. Furthermore, the art of workplaces continuing to work even with or without the workforce is to act upon itself to birth a new force of idle creatures condemning themselves to never attenuate or believe in the understanding of their knowledge or further itself.

The human mind is a long object and the only thing it excels in is bringing to life easier ways to old tactics. Once made present these ideas then the mind is free of its own volition to a stop if not made aware, then what reasoning has the mind to change for themselves or others? The workforce creates the means to supply colon drinks, cars, repairs etc. While it is the idle market who are creating demand for more of that product to stop it is an endless cycle that will always need two hands, or parties, to contribute to its rotation.

In the mid to late 20th century a man, Jean Shepherd, who ran a late-night radio show was extremely annoyed with the New York people as they did not care for anything unless it had an award, or nominee or was listed in the New York Times bestseller list.

Jean Shepherd asked his listeners late at night one time, when his view rate was at its lowest, to go into a bookstore the next day and ask for a book called I, Libertine. The book did not exist. Frederick R. Ewing, the pretentious name of the fake writer who had proclaimed the author, was to appear in magazines, newspapers, and radio show articles despite never existing, to begin with. Once creating a fake demand, booksellers would call the distributors and the distributors would then further contact the mega stores and, in due time, the media, which I used to respect, would catch wind of the subject and add it to their lists.

It had become such the talk of the town that everyone was born gifted a right by their universe or nature to have an opinion on the subject despite it never existing. Famously, a group of women were at a book party when the hostess brought up the subject of Ewing the other two women said that not only had they already read the book, but that one of them did not like it for stop

Phenomena is something we are all akin to in some respect, but this is the phenomenon of cognitive dissonance. The act of making it seem you know something purely to impress others. It is this deep neglect of the considerations that causes the means for the Profit Booking margin to continue despite it being, if not seen by, a complete book of morals, ethics and pure self-recognition in respect.

Ideas, search as I, libertine were created on two different grounds, the first is to expose the media listings for what they are and that is biased lists involving famous books/movies only famous due to their creators or connections. The second is to expose the ideals and unbounded morality of the people of New York, or any other City, and in turn of the world for stopping though this book was falsely made, and that is to say falsely as in was never made, to expose these atrocious husks for the reading, critiquing, and trend following they were and without actions or cause, will continue to be. But though the fake book was written, or not written, in Profit Booking style with a falsely pretentious author name and the fake title being pretentious in its wave, it was written with the sole ideals of exposure to the media and people who funded it, rather than the Profit Book of a mister full-stop Ewing. later Mr. Shepherd who created the book came out and stated that it was indeed fake and that everyone who had declared to have read it was lying all of the papers and magazines which claimed to have interviewed him or had insights on the next book were lying two: firstly, putting an end to the game Gene was playing.

Out of the many things and unnecessary atrocities in the world, both past and present, it seems that the ideas and thoughts behind Profit Book are to always be as they are. But it is from the works of Jean Shepherd that we can minimize the risk of Profit-Booking ideals in the papers we read and from the world we live in. Absurdism states that the world is without intrinsic meaning and so it only hurts the self if actions are performed unethically and without thought for their causes. And so, when people have little self-respect then they are to see little effect except for profits and fame when they submit Profit Books for stop and the Motives to determine a person's ethics and morals begin in school.

CHAPTER 20
The Universal Education System

Concerning the statement that was given in the last chapter, it is of essential importance to evaluate and speculate the meanings given.

Firstly man is to be condemned by the laws of duty and virtue of birth to be free. First, that is to be man and man is human. From that the people can understand that it is the universal school system where the problems of literary learning and recollection begin their sparks of misunderstanding and the abuse of words.

With students graded and taught in batches, and a good system for factory workers, not creatives, we are faced with the problem of adverse it when it comes to individual expression for stop many will have to find it necessary to complete their education which must result in them being able to see the attention of their work for passing grade at the very minimum sectors of their craft. though it is from this that many profit but books are born as they begin and continue to see these grades as their tickets as it were to a future in literary craft, which it could be, but most likely will not be. Instead, the grade they are given is a reflection of their work against their peers and level of skill set. It is also here that they're timing, and length diagrams are written in their minds.

Secondly, with only being given a few hours to complete a task, this is what will be grounded in them as an adequate length surfacing their minds to see themselves completing a short story or essay in a day or two or at most a week and believing that it is of an adequate state for publication, though it is in reality only being enough for a passing grade in secondary school English studies.

A basis for what is and is not adequate for publication is also seen by the education system. Students, or pupils as they should be called are an individual who wants to learn while the majority of state educators are forced pupils; pupated never hand back their works, be it a short story an essay or an entire novel, and given a truly critical analysis of it as this will only cause an uprise of the standard of work for the teacher. This should not be contrived as lazy though. A true critique of a pupil's work will see the teacher through at the very least an hour of their life. This multiplied by the amount of students they oversee subjects them to sleepless nights and, above all, they are not paid to care. The teacher is not paid to oversee and criticise a pupil's work. A teacher is paid from the start of a school day and is cut off at the end. Though small criticisms are given, if the pupil wishes - which they most likely will not - if the pupil wishes for their work to be overseen by a full critical analysis: then they will fund it with their reserve.

Above all, if the board of education truly saw to upgrade and excel the future of literary academia: taxes would be spent in wiser ways and seen to finding themselves on the desks of educators rather than those of rebates and unnecessary parades for unimportant persons. This is the final reason. And these three reasons given are never to stand purely for literature or artistic movements, but for all. We must see change as not arguing but rather a selfless task for which we know the bounties of which we will never know.

Their grades are not enough. A true critical analysis of facts, grammar and flow is needed with full participation from both the pupil and teacher to attain literary prowess. Prejudice, in a word, from the United Kingdom state government in matters of artistic education: prejudice. Prejudice to the arts, freedom and liberty in trifecta. The zenith of freedom is the arts and so is it the pillars. If it were to fall and be stricken by the hand that mocks and the hand that feeds, not only would the structural integrity of society crumble but also would it not destroy any chance of revival from the flame of literary liberties?

«END»

BIBLIOGRAPHY

Lovell, Stephen, *The Russian Reading Revolution*, Palgrave Macmillan London, London, 2000.

Schopenhauer, Arthur, *On Authorship And Style, Essays And Aphorisms*, Penguin Random House, London, 2004. The Project Gutenberg, 20th December 2022.
  <https://www.gutenberg.org/files/11945/11945-h/11945-h.htm#link2H_4_0004>

Callan, Matthew, *The Man Behind the Brilliant Hoax of I'Libertine*, The AWL, February 2013.
  <https://www.theawl.com/2013/02/the-man-behind-the-brilliant-media-hoax-of-i-libertine/>

Putney, James, *I, Libertine (1955)*, The Museum of Hoaxes, June 2018
  <http://hoaxes.org/archive/permalink/i_libertine>

Walker, Gregory, Soviet Book Publishing Policy, Cambridge Publications, 1980.

Cremona, Patrick, *Tetris true story: The game's creator on the real events behind the film*, Radio Times, March 2023.
https://www.radiotimes.com/movies/tetris-true-story-exclusive/

Wittgenstein, Ludwig, *Tractatus Logico-philosophicus,* Penguin Random House, London, 1922.

Moran Cioran, Emil, *On the Heights of Despair*, University of Chicago Press, Chicago, 1996.